Take a Deep Breath

little lessons from flowers
for a happier world

Written by
Allison Stoutland

Illustrated by
Cathy Hofher

inch by inch
PUBLICATIONS

Be like the flower,
turn your faces to the sun.
– Kahlil Gibran

————————————— • —————————————

We wish to extend
"bouquets" of thanks
to the following people who have advised, supported,
and encouraged us as we created
TAKE A DEEP BREATH:
Kathy Critser, Ann Flynn, Pam and Mark Bertilrud;
the many teachers and school children who inspire
and energize us; and, as always, our husbands,
children, sisters, brothers, and parents!
To our many friends who are also
married to football coaches,
we dedicate the lesson of the dandelion!

Published by
INCH BY INCH PUBLICATIONS, LLC
www.inchbyinchbooks.com

Library of Congress Catalog Card Number: 2002109748
ISBN 0-9670941-2-7

To my sister Karen,
whose constant support
keeps me growing!
— a.j.s.

In memory of Julia Caspary,
who loved flowers,
books, and friends.
— c.h.

The crocus taught me...

to lead by example.

Daffodils
taught me...

that winter will always melt into spring.

Tulips
taught me...

that lots of colors make the world more beautiful.

Buttercups
taught me...

how wonderful it is to help others shine.

Lilacs
taught me...

to take a deep breath!

Forget-me-nots

taught me...

to remember others.

Sunflowers taught me...

... unique.

to be proud of what makes me

Dandelions
taught me...

to appreciate life no matter where it takes me.

Hollyhocks
taught me...

that everyone can use a little support now and then.

Roses

taught me...

how to handle

. with care.

Daisies
taught me...

that sometimes they'll love me and sometimes they won't.

Pansies
taught me...

Chrysanthemums
taught me...

that summer will always settle into fall.

My garden
taught me...

that we can all live together.

inch by inch
PUBLICATIONS

www.inchbyinchbooks.com